Friedrich Kuhlau

Complete Sonatinas

DOVER PUBLICATIONS, INC.
Mineola, New York

Bibliographical Note

Complete Sonatinas, first published by Dover Publications, Inc., in 2008, is an unabridged republication of the edition originally published by G. Shirmer, Inc., in 1893.

International Standard Book Number
ISBN-13: 978-0-486-46907-2
ISBN-10: 0-486-46907-7

Manufactured in the United States by LSC Communications
46907703   2020
www.doverpublications.com

CONTENTS

Sonatina in C Major

Friedrich Kuhlau
Op. 20, No. 1

a) These small slurs indicate that the last bass-note in one measure should be carefully connected with the first bass-note in the next.

Sonatina in G Major

Friedrich Kuhlau
Op. 20, No. 2

Adagio e sostenuto

10 Allegro scherzando

a) Strike the appoggiatura simultaneously with the accompaniment.

Sonatina in F Major

Friedrich Kuhlau
Op. 20, No. 3

Allegro con spirito

a) [notation] b) Strike the appoggiatura. *f.* simultaneously with the notes for the right hand, *d* and *a*. c)

Allegro Polacca

Sonatina in C Major

Friedrich Kuhlau
Op. 55, No. 1

*) Remark: These small slurs indicate that the last bass-note in one measure should be carefully connected with the first bass-note in the next.

21

Sonatina in G Major

Friedrich Kuhlau
Op. 55, No. 2

*) Remark: These small slurs indicate that the last bass-note in one measure should be carefully connected with the first bass-note in the next.

24

Sonatina in C Major

Friedrich Kuhlau
Op. 55, No. 3

*) **Remark:** These small slurs indicate that the last bass-note in one measure should be carefully connected with the first bass-note in the next.

Allegretto grazioso

29

Sonatina in F Major

Friedrich Kuhlau
Op. 55, No. 4

*) Remark: These small slurs indicate that the last bass-note in one measure should be carefully connected with the first bass-note in the next. a) ... b) like a.

Andante con espressione

Alla Polacca

Sonatina in D Major

Friedrich Kuhlau
Op. 55, No. 5

Tempo di Marcia

*) **Remark:** These small slurs indicate that the last bass-note in one measure should be **carefully** connected with the first bass-note in the next.

Vivace assai

Sonatina in C Major

Friedrich Kuhlau
Op. 55, No. 6

Allegro **maestoso**

c) like a.) d) like b.)

Menuet

p legato.

cresc.

44

Trio

Men. D.C. senza replica, e poi la Coda

Coda

Sonatina in A Major

Friedrich Kuhlau
Op. 59, No. 1

Rondo

Allegro scherzando

Sonatina in F Major

Friedrich Kuhlau
Op. 59, No. 2

Rondo
Allegro

Sonatina in C Major

Friedrich Kuhlau
Op. 59, No. 3

Allegro con spirito

64

a)

Rondo

Allegro vivace

68

70

(This page has been left intentionally blank.)

Sonatina in F Major

Friedrich Kuhlau
Op. 60, No. 1

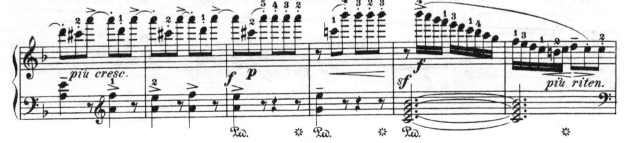

Tema
(Rossini)

Var.2.

Var.4.

Sonatina in A Major

Friedrich Kuhlau
Op. 60, No. 2

Allegro con spirito

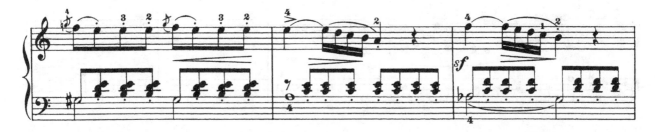

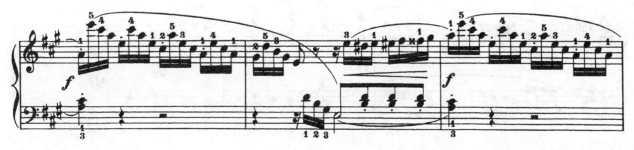

Allegro moderato

Tema
(Rossini)

Var.1

Poco agitato

Var. 3

Sonatina in C Major

Friedrich Kuhlau
Op. 60, No. 3

Allegro vivace

Tema
(Rossini)

Var. 1

Meno Allegro

Var.3

(This page has been left intentionally blank.)

Sonatina in C Major

Friedrich Kuhlau
Op. 88, No. 1

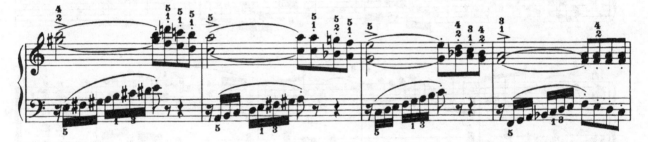

Andantino

dolce con espressione

(a)

Rondo
Allegro

(a)

Sonatina in G Major

Friedrich Kuhlau
Op. 88, No. 2

108

Andante cantabile

Rondo
Vivace

110

Sonatina in A minor

Friedrich Kuhlau
Op. 88, No. 3

Allegro con affetto

Andantino

a tempo.

Allegro burlesco

Sonatina in F Major

Friedrich Kuhlau
Op. 88, No. 4

Allegro molto